The Orchestra of Ordinary Things

Symphony of the Everyday

Holly Clark

Chapter 1: The Morning Overture

First Lights Awakening

The gentle hum of dawn crept through the gossamer curtains, painting Sarah's bedroom walls in soft amber hues. Her consciousness stirred before the alarm could announce its daily intrusion. In these precious moments between sleep and wakefulness, she discovered a symphony that had always existed, yet remained unnoticed until now.

The radiator clicked its morning morse code, a rhythmic pattern that seemed to speak in a language just beyond comprehension. Sarah lay still, allowing her ears to tune into the world's awakening orchestra. Outside, the earliest birds began their overture – not the full chorus of daylight, but the solo performers who dared to break the night's silence.

Her neighbor's car purred to life three houses down, its engine adding a bass note to the emerging composition. The sound traveled through the quiet street, bouncing off frost-kissed windows and weathered brick walls. A distant train whistle joined in, its mournful call echoing across the valley, carrying stories of travelers and dreams in transit.

Sarah's fingers traced patterns on her cotton sheets, each fiber creating microscopic whispers. The house itself seemed to breathe, expanding and contracting with the warming air. Wooden beams adjusted their ancient joints, contributing creaks and groans to the morning's arrangement.

Through her half-open window, the scent of dew-laden grass drifted in, accompanied by the subtle rustle of leaves responding to the day's first breeze. The wind chimes in Mrs. Peterson's garden next door added their crystalline voices, a delicate counterpoint to the steady rhythm of the awakening world.

As consciousness fully embraced her, Sarah began to understand why she had been chosen. The letter she had received yesterday still lay on her nightstand, its official letterhead bearing the mysterious insignia of the Ordinary Symphony Society. They had identified her ability – this gift of hearing the music in the mundane, of finding harmony in the everyday chaos that most people dismissed as noise.

She reached for the letter, its paper crinkling with possibility. The society's invitation was clear: become their newest conductor, help others discover the hidden melodies threading through their lives. But first, she would need to master her own daily symphony.

Rolling onto her side, Sarah watched dust motes dance in the strengthening sunbeams. They moved like notes floating off an invisible score, each particle playing its part in an airborne ballet. The central heating system joined the performance, its initial grumble softening into a steady drone that underpinned the morning's growing composition.

Her cat, Mozart, stretched on the windowsill, his purr adding a gentle vibrato to the ensemble. His tail twitched in time with the ticking clock, creating a visual metronome for the room's ongoing concert. Sarah smiled, remembering how she had named him long before discovering her gift, as if some part of her had always known about the music hiding in plain sight.

Beyond her walls, the world's tempo increased. Car doors slammed in syncopated rhythm, children's voices carried on the morning air like scattered wind instruments, and somewhere, a lawn mower grumbled to life, its mechanical drone a persistent ostinato in the distance.

The letter had warned her that once she accepted her role, there would be no returning to the ordinary way of hearing things. Each day would become an immersive symphony, each moment laden with potential melodies. The responsibility felt heavy yet exciting – like holding the score to an infinite composition.

Sarah swung her legs out of bed, her bare feet meeting the cool floorboards. Even this simple contact produced a note in her mind, a gentle percussion that would begin her day's movement. She stood, ready to conduct her first conscious symphony, understanding that this morning marked the beginning of something extraordinary.

The sun now painted bold strokes across her room, transforming shadows into dancing partners and turning everyday objects into instruments waiting to be played. Sarah took a deep breath, allowing the morning air to fill her lungs with possibility. She was no longer just an observer of the daily orchestra – she was becoming its conductor, ready to help others hear the extraordinary music in their ordinary lives.

As she moved toward her window, the floorboards singing beneath her steps, Sarah embraced her new reality. The morning's awakening had become more than just a daily routine; it was the opening movement of an endless symphony, one that had always been playing, waiting for someone to finally listen.

Steam Rising Symphony

Sarah's kettle whistled its morning solo, sending spirals of steam dancing through the kitchen air. Since discovering her gift of hearing the music in everyday sounds, this simple act of brewing tea had transformed into an intimate concert. The rising vapor created visible notes that swirled and twisted, conducting their own ethereal melody.

Standing in her small kitchen, she closed her eyes and listened to the water's transformation. The initial bubbling began as a soft pianissimo, growing steadily into a rolling boil that reminded her of timpani drums building to a crescendo. The steam escaped in rhythmic puffs, each release adding its voice to the morning's performance.

Through the window above her sink, she noticed her neighbors' homes releasing their own steam symphonies – shower vapor escaping through vents, dryer exhaust creating puffy clouds, and breakfast preparations sending wisps of cooking steam into the cool morning air. Each source contributed its unique timbre to the neighborhood's growing composition.

The Ordinary Symphony Society's letter had mentioned this phenomenon – how steam carried sound waves differently, how its very movement created music that most people dismissed as mere background noise. Sarah found herself conducting with her teaspoon, directing the steam's path as it rose from her cup. Each swirl responded to her movement, creating visible sound waves that only she could hear.

Her bathroom mirror, still foggy from her shower, held traces of this morning's earlier steam symphony. She had drawn musical notes in the condensation, watching as they slowly faded like disappearing ink. The humidity in the air carried the echoes of water droplets falling from her hair, each one contributing a crystalline ping to the ongoing composition.

The radiator in the corner joined the performance, its steam heat creating a sustained bass note that underscored the higher pitches of the kettle and shower. Sarah remembered her grandmother's old steam radiator, how its clanking and hissing had frightened her as a child. Now she understood – it had been trying to sing all along.

Outside, a steam cleaner roared to life as Mr. Jenkins began his weekly ritual of washing his driveway. The machine's powerful jets released clouds that caught the morning light, transforming into visible sound waves that rippled through the air. Sarah watched through her kitchen window as the steam created temporary sculptures, each one holding a note before dissipating into the atmosphere.

The society's training manual sat open on her counter, its pages describing the different types of steam songs – the sharp staccato of espresso machines, the lengthy legato of industrial smokestacks, the gentle vibrato of clothes steamers. Sarah had begun categorizing them in her notebook, creating a taxonomy of steam-based sounds that would help her teach others to hear what she could.

Her tea had cooled enough to drink, but the mug still released gentle wisps that played like woodwind instruments in her mind. Each sip created its own miniature performance – the steam rising from the liquid's surface, the warm breath she exhaled, the condensation forming and evaporating on the ceramic surface.

The morning's humidity wrapped around her like an embrace, carrying the collective steam symphony of countless households beginning their days. Somewhere, a pressure cooker released its steam in a powerful burst, adding an unexpected percussion to the neighborhood's soundtrack. A dry cleaning facility down the street contributed its industrial harmonies, its massive steamers creating deep, resonant tones that traveled through the morning air.

Sarah opened her kitchen window wider, allowing the steam from her kettle to meet the cool outdoor air. The collision created tiny vortexes that spun like music box dancers, each one carrying a fragment of melody into the world. She thought about how many people would walk through these notes today, never knowing they were part of an ongoing concert.

The society had chosen her for this gift – the ability to hear the music in steam's dance, to understand the songs carried in water's gaseous form. As she prepared for another day of discovery, Sarah realized that steam was perhaps the most visible of all the ordinary music surrounding her. It made the invisible visible, turning mundane moments into magical ones.

Her teacup now empty, Sarah watched the last wisps of steam rise and fade. Even in their disappearance, they left behind a lingering note, a promise of more music to come. She gathered her things, ready to step into a world where every puff of steam, every cloud of vapor, every humid breath carried its own melody, waiting for someone to stop and listen.

The steam rising symphony continued around her, an endless performance of transformation and release, each molecule a musician in the great orchestra of the everyday.

Breakfast Percussion

Sarah arranged her breakfast items on the kitchen counter with the precision of a percussionist setting up their instruments. The ceramic bowl clinked against the granite countertop, establishing the first note of the morning's culinary concert. Since receiving her invitation from the Ordinary Symphony Society, breakfast had become more than a meal – it was a performance.

The cereal box shook in her hands like a rain stick, granola cascading into the bowl in a steady rhythm. Each piece struck the ceramic surface with a different pitch, creating a natural scale that descended as the bowl filled. She remembered the society's manual describing how ancient cultures used dried grains in their percussion instruments, finding music in their daily sustenance.

Her spoon struck the bowl's edge accidentally, producing a clear, bell-like tone that hung in the air. The sound reminded her of temple bells, and she smiled, realizing that her breakfast table had become its own sacred space of musical discovery. The refrigerator door opened with a satisfying percussion of shifting containers and clinking glass bottles.

Pouring milk created a new layer of sound – first, the bottle's seal cracking like a snare drum, then the liquid streaming into the bowl, striking the cereal in a syncopated pattern. The pitch changed as the bowl filled, rising from a deep resonance to a higher tone. Small splashes added cymbal-like accents to the milk's steady pour.

At the counter next to her, the coffee maker performed its morning ritual. Water dripped in steady eighth notes, steam escaped in airy whispers, and the carafe occasionally popped as it heated. Sarah had learned to distinguish between the different stages of brewing by sound alone – the initial gurgle of water heating, the pressurized burst as it reached the grounds, the steady drip-drip-drip of filtered coffee.

Her toast popped up with a metallic spring sound, launching into the morning air like a jumping percussion note. Butter spread across the warm surface with soft, brushing sounds reminiscent of jazz brushes on a snare drum. The knife clinked against the plate as she set it down, adding another tone to the breakfast symphony.

Across the street, she could hear her neighbor's breakfast percussion through an open window – the whir of a blender creating a sustained roll, the clash of pots and pans like cymbals in an orchestra, the rhythmic chopping of vegetables on a cutting board. Each household contributed its own section to the neighborhood's morning ensemble.

Sarah's spoon moved through the cereal, creating waves of crunching sounds that reminded her of footsteps in fresh snow. The society had taught her that texture in food created its own particular music – soft foods produced gentle sustained notes, while crispy foods offered sharp, staccato beats. Her breakfast was a combination of both, a duet between crunch and smooth.

The dishwasher from last night's dinner finished its cycle with a series of clicks and hisses, like a percussion section winding down after a complex piece. Water drained through pipes in the wall, adding a deep, resonant bass note to the kitchen's ongoing composition. Even the dish rack contributed its part as wet plates slowly dripped, each drop striking the metal sink in perfect time.

Her phone vibrated against the counter, its buzz creating a mechanical tremolo that skittered across the surface. Sarah let it continue, appreciating how its rhythm complemented the morning's acoustic instruments. Modern sounds had their place in this ancient symphony of breakfast preparation.

As she ate, each bite created its own small percussion session – the crunch of cereal, the clink of spoon against bowl, the subtle sound of swallowing that added a human element to the performance. She had learned to appreciate these intimate sounds, understanding that they connected her to every other person starting their day with similar rituals.

The last drops of coffee fell into the carafe with diminishing volume, like the final notes of a performed piece. Sarah poured the coffee into her favorite mug, the stream of liquid creating yet another percussion line in the morning's score. Steam rose from the surface in visible waves, carrying the aroma that seemed to dance in time with the kitchen's symphony.

Finishing her breakfast, Sarah collected her dishes with careful attention to each sound they made. The bowl and spoon settled into the sink with a gentle clash, water from the faucet provided a flowing backdrop, and the sponge squeaked against ceramic in rhythm with her cleaning motions. Even this simple act of washing up had become part of the greater percussion performance of her morning routine.

The breakfast percussion section of her day complete, Sarah dried her hands on a towel that swished softly, a gentle cymbal crash to conclude the movement. She gathered her belongings, each item adding its own note to her departure – keys jingling, bag zipping, door closing with a solid thump. The morning's domestic symphony would continue in kitchens across the city, an endless percussion concert of everyday life.

Morning News Chorus

The rustling of newspaper pages filled Sarah's living room like leaves dancing in an autumn breeze. Since joining the Ordinary Symphony Society, she had discovered that even the daily news created its own unique musical composition. Each page turn contributed a different note to the morning's paper symphony, from the deep bass of the heavy front page to the lighter treble of the lifestyle section.

Her father had always said that newspapers were dying, replaced by digital screens and silent scrolling. But here, in the early morning light, the physical paper proved itself very much alive – singing its stories through tactile percussion and papery whispers. The sound of pages shifting reminded her of orchestra members adjusting their sheet music before a performance.

Coffee steam rose from her mug, accompanying the soft crinkle of newsprint as she smoothed out wrinkled corners. Headlines seemed to project themselves with bold fortissimo, while smaller articles whispered their contents in pianissimo tones. Sarah noticed how different sections of the paper produced distinct sounds – the glossy magazine inserts sliding against each other like silk strings, while the coarse business pages rustled with authority.

Through her open window, she heard her neighbor's radio announcing the morning news. The broadcaster's voice carried across the garden, merging with her newspaper's acoustic performance. Electronic and paper media performed an unexpected duet, proving that old and new could harmonize rather than compete.

The society's training had taught her to recognize the subtle variations in paper quality. The local newspaper's slightly rough texture created a different timbre than the smooth national broadsheets. Advertising inserts added their own bright notes to the mixture, their shiny surfaces creating sharp, clear tones when handled.

Sarah's fingers drummed unconsciously on the paper as she read, adding a gentle percussion to the news chorus. The sound reminded her of rain on a tin roof – each fingertip contributing its own small voice to the rhythm. She had begun to notice how other readers created their own unique music: some flicked pages impatiently, producing sharp staccato notes, while others turned them slowly, drawing out each sound like a sustained chord.

A gust of wind through the window caught several pages, making them flutter like wings. The unexpected movement created an improvisational section in the morning's performance – a free-form jazz solo of paper and air. Sarah caught the pages, smoothing them back into place, the paper responding with soft sighs of submission.

Her cat Mozart jumped onto the table, adding his purring bass line to the composition. His paws padded across the business section, creating soft thuds that punctuated stock market reports and economic forecasts. A particularly interesting bird outside caused his tail to twitch against the sports pages, adding an unplanned percussion element.

The crossword puzzle crackled as she folded the paper precisely, creating sharp creases that sang with geometric precision. Her pencil scratched against the surface, adding another layer to the morning's soundtrack. Each solved clue was accompanied by the satisfying sound of graphite meeting newsprint, a tiny celebration of mental victory.

In the distance, a newspaper delivery van's doors slammed, sending more scores of potential music to other homes in the neighborhood. Sarah imagined all the different ways these papers would be read – spread across breakfast tables, folded for commuter trains, shared between coffee shop patrons. Each reader would create their own unique arrangement of the morning news chorus.

The opinion pages sparked a particularly vigorous rustle as she disagreed with an editorial, the paper seeming to share her agitation through its increased volume. She had noticed how emotional responses changed the way people handled newspapers – anger led to sharp, loud movements, while contemplation produced softer, more measured sounds.

Classified advertisements whispered their secrets in small, delicate movements. Wedding announcements rang out with joy in crisp, clean folds, while obituaries seemed to carry a heavier, more somber tone in their darker ink and quieter handling. Every section told its stories not just through words, but through the sounds of their discovery.

As she reached the final pages, Sarah noticed how the paper had transformed through her reading – from its initial crisp orchestra to a more relaxed, well-handled ensemble. Dog-eared corners marked interesting articles, creating permanent changes in the paper's acoustic properties. Even these imperfections added character to the morning's performance.

Setting aside the completed paper, she listened to it settle – a few last whispers as pages found their resting places. Tomorrow would bring a new edition, a fresh symphony of news and noise, stories and sounds. The morning news chorus would play again, each day unique yet familiar, part of the greater orchestra of ordinary life that the society had taught her to hear and appreciate.

Footsteps to the Door

Sarah's ears perked up at the first distant tap of heels against pavement, a sound that marked the beginning of her neighbor's daily journey to work. Since the Ordinary Symphony Society had awakened her to the music of everyday life, the morning parade of footsteps had become her favorite urban symphony.

Each pair of shoes created its own distinct melody. Heavy work boots drummed steady, confident rhythms, while sneakers whispered soft, syncopated patterns across the concrete. High heels performed their staccato solos, clicking precise eighth notes that echoed between buildings. The morning's composition built gradually as more residents emerged from their homes, each adding their unique footfall to the growing ensemble.

Through her open window, she tracked the different tempos of her neighbors' walks. Mr. Johnson from apartment 3B always rushed, his dress shoes creating a allegro rhythm that suggested perpetual lateness. Mrs. Chen moved more deliberately, her gentle footsteps forming a peaceful andante as she headed to her morning tai chi practice in the park.

The weather influenced the symphony significantly. Today's dry morning produced clear, crisp sounds, but Sarah recalled how yesterday's rain had transformed the sidewalk into a percussion section of splashes and squeaks. Winter brought the muffled harmonies of snow-covered steps, while autumn contributed the crunch of fallen leaves under foot.

Children's footsteps played their own special part in the morning orchestra. They skipped, jumped, and ran, creating playful arpeggios that contrasted with the more measured walks of adults. The twins from the building next door always raced to the school bus, their synchronized footfalls performing an energetic duet that made Sarah smile.

The society's training had taught her to distinguish between the different surfaces people traversed. Concrete provided a solid, resonant foundation, while metal grating added industrial overtones. The wooden steps of front porches contributed warm, organic notes, and the marble lobby of her building amplified every step into a miniature concert hall.

Dogs added their own four-beat rhythms to the morning symphony. Their claws clicked against the pavement in rapid sequences, sometimes breaking into sudden accelerandos when squirrels appeared. The elderly golden retriever from the corner house maintained a slow, dignified pace, his heavy paws marking time like a metronome.

Sarah noticed how footsteps changed when people approached their destinations. Steps quickened near bus stops, creating crescendos of urgency. They slowed and softened near the café, where the scent of coffee drew people into a more relaxed tempo. The post office steps always seemed purposeful and measured, while those approaching the park became lighter, more carefree.

Groups created their own complex rhythms. The morning running club passed by in a swift chorus of rubber soles, while the high school students walked in clusters, their footsteps merging and separating like jazz improvisations. Couples often fell into synchronized patterns, their steps harmonizing naturally as they walked together.

The mail carrier's route was a daily recurring theme in the neighborhood's foot symphony. His steady pace provided a baseline rhythm, punctuated by brief pauses at each mailbox. The heavy bag of letters and packages added weight to his steps, creating deeper tones that gradually lightened as his deliveries progressed.

Construction workers arrived with their steel-toed orchestration, their heavy boots providing a strong foundation for the day's urban soundtrack. The crossing guard's pivoting feet conducted the ebb and flow of pedestrian traffic, her movements creating regular intervals in the morning's composition.

Sarah had learned to recognize regular passersby by their footsteps alone. The newspaper delivery person's quick, efficient pace arrived first, followed by the baker's flour-dusted boots heading to the corner patisserie. The nurse from the night shift returned with tired steps, while the yoga instructor seemed to float past, barely disturbing the morning air.

Different seasons brought different ensembles of walkers. Summer welcomed sandals that slapped cheerfully against heels, while spring introduced new runners with their enthusiastic gaits. The first frost drove boots out of storage, adding deeper tones to the sidewalk symphony.

As the morning peaked, the footstep orchestra reached its fullest expression. Hundreds of individual rhythms merged into a complex urban score – a celebration of movement, purpose, and the simple act of going somewhere. Each step told a story: of commutes and errands, of meetings and partings, of routine and adventure.

The society had revealed to Sarah that footsteps were more than just noise – they were the heartbeat of city life, the rhythm section of humanity's daily dance. Every morning brought a new arrangement of this eternal symphony, a unique combination of paces, paths, and purposes expressed through the simple act of walking from here to there.

The morning's parade of footsteps gradually thinned as people reached their destinations, but Sarah knew the symphony would continue throughout the day. New performers would join, others would exit, but the music of movement would play on, step by step, in the great orchestra of ordinary life.

Chapter 2: Workplace Ensemble

The Digital Orchestra

Electronic devices filled Sarah's home office with their subtle symphony, a modern orchestra that the Ordinary Symphony Society had taught her to appreciate. Her laptop hummed a steady baseline, its cooling fan adjusting speed like a responsive percussion section. The external hard drive added its own rhythmic pulse, data spinning and storing in measured beats.

Each notification brought a unique tone to the composition. Email alerts chimed like tiny triangles in an orchestra, while calendar reminders sounded deeper, more insistent notes. Text messages created short, bright accents that punctuated the ongoing digital performance. Even the silent vibration of her phone contributed a physical rhythm to the electronic ensemble.

The printer warmed up with a series of mechanical movements, its internal gears and rollers creating an intricate mechanical ballet. Paper fed through with a whisper, followed by the precise dance of ink heads moving left and right, laying down their patterns in steady sweeps. Each completed page dropped into the tray with a soft percussion note.

Her wireless mouse glided across the desk pad, its optical sensor tracking movement with invisible precision. The subtle clicks of right and left buttons added quiet percussion, while the scroll wheel contributed gentle rolls like a tiny rainmaker instrument. The mechanical keyboard responded with satisfying clacks, each key producing a slightly different tone based on its position and purpose.

Network activity lights blinked in patterns that reminded Sarah of a conductor's baton, directing the flow of data through invisible airways. The router's steady glow provided a constant presence, like stage lights illuminating the performance. Occasional flurries of activity sent the lights into rapid sequences, creating visual rhythms that matched the increased data flow.

The UPS battery backup hummed its low, reassuring note, protecting the entire electronic orchestra from power fluctuations. Its occasional self-test sequence played like a brief solo, checking each component with methodical precision. The surge protector strip lay silent until needed, ready to defend against electrical storms with its hidden capacitors and circuits.

Sarah's smartwatch tracked her heartbeat, adding a biological rhythm to the digital symphony. Its haptic feedback created gentle taps against her wrist, marking time and delivering messages in morse-code-like patterns. The health monitoring apps contributed their own data streams, translating physical movement into digital rhythms.

The room's smart lighting responded to the time of day, gradually shifting color temperature in subtle progressions. Each adjustment was accompanied by barely perceptible electronic whispers as the LEDs changed their output. The smart thermostat clicked softly as it maintained the room's climate, its display glowing with changing numbers like a minimalist score.

Video calls brought distant voices into the space, each compressed and reconstructed through speakers that added their own acoustic signatures. Microphones captured and transmitted sound in continuous streams, while webcams hummed quietly, their focus motors making microscopic adjustments. The digital signal processor worked invisibly to clean and enhance these audio streams, conducting its own silent symphony of algorithms.

Cloud storage services synchronized in the background, their activity indicated by small progress bars and occasional status messages. Each completed upload or download was marked with a subtle sound, like cymbal taps in a larger composition. File compression processes added bursts of CPU activity, the processor's cooling fan responding with corresponding crescendos.

The solid-state drive performed its data ballet in complete silence, but its activity light flickered in complex patterns that suggested the intricate choreography of bits and bytes. RAM modules pulsed with electricity, their nanosecond timing creating rhythms too fast for human perception but vital to the overall performance.

Background processes created their own layers of activity – system updates checking for new versions, security software scanning for threats, backup programs ensuring data safety. Each contributed to the overall load on the system, influencing the tempo and intensity of the digital orchestra's performance.

Sarah's tablet chimed as it finished charging, its tone marking the completion of one electronic cycle and the beginning of another. The wireless charging pad beneath it generated subtle electromagnetic frequencies, an invisible conductor directing the flow of power. Even the power supplies transformed electrical current with barely audible frequencies, their components singing quiet songs of voltage conversion.

The internet connection itself added an unseen dimension to the performance, packets of data flowing in precisely timed intervals. Network protocols conducted their careful dance of handshakes and acknowledgments, maintaining the complex choreography of modern connectivity. Error correction routines caught and repaired data transmission flaws like attentive section leaders in an orchestra.

As evening approached, the digital orchestra began its gradual diminuendo. Programs closed with their signature sound effects, save dialogs appeared with gentle prompts, and systems prepared for sleep modes. The backup process initiated its nightly routine, a final flourish of activity before the system settled into its quieter nighttime rhythm.

The society had revealed to Sarah that these electronic sounds weren't just technical necessities – they were the music of modern life, a complex and coordinated performance of human innovation. Each device, each process, each digital interaction contributed its voice

to an ever-evolving symphony of technology and
purpose.

Corridor Harmonies

Footsteps echoed through the marble-floored hallway
of Sarah's apartment building, each resident
contributing their unique voice to the corridor's daily
concert. Since joining the Ordinary Symphony
Society, she had discovered that these shared spaces
created their own distinct musical compositions,
blending the sounds of community life into an ever-
changing symphony.

The morning rush hour brought the most dynamic
performance, as neighbors hurried to their daily
commitments. Doors opened and closed in various
rhythms – some with confident thuds, others with
gentle clicks. Keys jingled like tiny cymbals, creating
metallic accents in the corridor's acoustic space. The
elevator chimed its ascending and descending notes,
marking the movement of residents between floors.

Children's voices carried differently in the hallway
than adults', their higher frequencies bouncing off the
walls in playful patterns. The Martinez twins from the
third floor always raced to the stairs, their footsteps
creating rapid staccato passages that reverberated
through the building. Their mother's calls for them to
slow down added deeper notes to the morning
composition.

The mail carrier's daily visit brought a reliable
sequence of sounds: the metallic clatter of the mailbox
panel opening, the soft thump of letters falling into

individual boxes, the rhythmic sorting of packages. These familiar sounds had become a cornerstone of the corridor's daily performance, as regular as a metronome marking time.

Weather changed the hallway's acoustics subtly but noticeably. Rainy days brought the squeak of wet shoes on marble and the shake of damp umbrellas. Winter added the swish of heavy coats and the thud of boots being stamped clean. Summer opened windows at each end of the corridor, allowing street sounds to drift in and mix with the interior symphony.

Rolling suitcases created their own distinctive music, wheels humming against the floor in long, sustained notes. Weekend travelers pulled smaller bags with quick, light rhythms, while vacation departures involved heavier luggage that rumbled more deeply. The sound of approaching wheels always told a story about the journey ahead.

The building's maintenance staff contributed their own instrumental sections to the corridor orchestra. The soft swish of brooms and mops provided a gentle backdrop, while the vacuum cleaner added its powerful drone on scheduled cleaning days. The superintendent's tool belt jingled as he made his rounds, each tool creating its own distinct tone.

Evening brought a different tempo to the corridor's composition. Dinner preparations sent aromatic harmonies drifting under doors, accompanied by the muffled sounds of cooking and conversation. Food delivery arrivals punctuated the night with quick knocks and brief exchanges, creating short movements in the ongoing symphony.

Pet owners added their own chapters to the corridor's score. Dogs' claws clicked against the floor in various rhythms, while cat carriers swung gently as their owners transported feline friends to vet appointments. The elderly Mrs. Peterson's parakeet could sometimes be heard singing through her door, adding unexpected solos to the hallway's acoustic environment.

The building's pipes and heating system provided a constant underlying harmony. Radiators hissed and clanked in winter, while air conditioning units hummed during summer months. These mechanical voices became so familiar that their absence was immediately noticeable, like missing instruments in an orchestra.

Package deliveries brought their own percussion section – the thump of boxes being set down, the scratch of pens on delivery forms, the crinkle of plastic envelopes. The varying sizes of deliveries created different tones, from the sharp tap of small parcels to the deep resonance of larger boxes.

Conversations in the corridor took on different characters depending on their location. Near the elevator, exchanges were brief and bright, while longer discussions by apartment doors had more measured, intimate tones. The acoustic properties of the space shaped these interactions, turning quick greetings into part of the building's social music.

Late nights brought their own quiet movement to the corridor symphony. The soft footsteps of residents returning from evening shifts, the gentle click of keys in locks, the distant sound of television programs or music floating through walls – all combined in a muted nocturne that played until dawn.

Special occasions transformed the corridor's usual composition. Holiday decorations added tinsel sounds and the crinkle of wrapping paper. Moving days brought the grunt and shuffle of furniture being transported, while party preparations filled the space with excited voices and the rustle of shopping bags.

The society had taught Sarah to appreciate how these corridor harmonies represented more than just random noise – they were the soundtrack of shared living, the music of community in motion. Each sound told a story about her neighbors' lives, their daily rhythms, their comings and goings. The corridor served as both concert hall and community space, where the music of ordinary life played its endless symphony.

As she listened to the evening's gentle diminuendo of returning residents and settling households, Sarah realized that these corridor harmonies were a unique form of music that could never be replicated in a concert hall. They were the authentic sound of human lives intersecting in shared space, creating an ever-changing composition of community life.

Meeting Room Concerto

Every workplace meeting room holds its own distinct musical composition, a fact Sarah discovered after joining the Ordinary Symphony Society. The large conference room on the fifteenth floor of her office building performed daily concerts of human interaction, corporate ritual, and technological harmony.

The prelude began each morning as the cleaning staff prepared the space. Chairs squeaked against the floor as they were perfectly aligned, creating a rhythmic pattern of plastic and metal. The gentle whir of the air conditioning system provided a constant drone, while the hum of fluorescent lights added their high-frequency notes to the ambient soundtrack.

Early meetings started with the percussion of laptop cases being placed on the polished table, followed by the clicking of power buttons and the soft whine of machines starting up. Participants arrived in waves, their footsteps varying from the confident stride of presenters to the hesitant pace of new employees. Coffee cups created gentle percussive sounds as they met the glass tabletop, occasionally accompanied by the rustle of pastry bags or the crack of water bottle caps being twisted open.

The projection system contributed its own overture – the mechanical whir of the screen descending, the warm-up hum of the projector, and the subtle electronic handshake between laptops and display equipment. Wireless keyboards added their quiet clicks to the preparation symphony, while mice glided across mousepads with barely perceptible friction sounds.

Phone conferences brought a unique layer to the acoustic environment. The speaker phone's ring tone announced remote participants, while the digital compression of voices through the system created distinctive timbres. The mute button's click became a conductor's signal, controlling the flow of conversation between physical and virtual spaces.

Document sharing created its own rhythm section – the shuffle of papers being distributed, the snap of presentation folders opening and closing, the scratch of pens on notepads. Digital presentations added their signature sounds: the soft tap of keyboard arrows advancing slides, the subtle beep of laser pointers being activated, the click of USB drives being inserted and removed.

The room's acoustics shaped every sound. Glass walls reflected voices differently than the carpeted floor absorbed them. The long oval table acted as a sounding board, carrying vibrations of tapped pens and placed objects. Even the leather chairs contributed their own notes, creaking and shifting as participants leaned forward or back during discussions.

Brainstorming sessions transformed the room's symphony with their unique energy. The squeak of markers on whiteboards, the stick-and-peel sound of Post-it notes being arranged and rearranged, the simultaneous murmur of small group discussions – all combined to create a different movement in the meeting room's ongoing composition.

Technical difficulties added unexpected solos to the performance. The projector's cooling fan would sometimes increase its tempo, creating an urgent drone that underscored technical support calls. Feedback from misaligned audio equipment could send sharp notes through the space, while dead batteries in wireless peripherals brought sudden silences to presentations.

The room's temperature control system played its own part in the concert. Vents opened and closed with subtle mechanical sounds, responding to the heat generated by equipment and occupants. The automatic blinds adjusted themselves throughout the day, their motors humming as they tracked the sun's movement across the sky.

Lunch meetings introduced a new movement to the daily symphony. The rustle of paper bags and plastic containers, the clink of utensils, the pop of soda cans being opened – these sounds created a midday intermezzo in the business day's composition. The subtle aroma of various foods added an invisible dimension to the sensory experience.

Different meeting styles brought different acoustic patterns. Board meetings carried formal rhythms of parliamentary procedure and measured responses. Team building exercises filled the space with more dynamic sounds – laughter, movement, the scrape of chairs being rearranged. Training sessions added the scratch of pencils during note-taking and the periodic chorus of questions from attendees.

The end of each meeting had its own closing movement. Laptops clicked shut in sequence, chairs pushed back in a scattered rhythm, and conversations faded into hallway echoes. Papers shuffled into briefcases, creating soft rustling finales to each session. The projector's cooling fan slowly wound down, like an orchestra's final diminuendo.

Between meetings, the room held moments of remarkable silence, broken only by the building's mechanical systems and the muffled sounds of office life beyond its walls. These quiet interludes served as rests between movements, preparing the space for its next performance.

The society had taught Sarah that meeting rooms were more than just functional spaces – they were concert halls for the music of modern business. Each gathering brought its unique arrangement of human voices, technical sounds, and ambient noise, creating an ever-changing symphony of professional life. The meeting room's daily concerts told stories of decisions made, ideas shared, and connections formed, all set to the subtle music of corporate collaboration.

Chapter 3: Domestic Harmonies

Kitchens Melodic Dance

Steam rose from the pot like musical notes floating in the air as Sarah stirred the simmering soup, each bubble creating its own percussive note against the stainless steel. The Ordinary Symphony Society had opened her ears to the intricate melodies that filled her kitchen, transforming everyday cooking into a orchestral experience.

The refrigerator provided a steady baseline, its compressor cycling on and off in measured intervals. Ice maker components shifted with occasional crystalline clicks, while the water dispenser added unexpected water-drop percussion to the kitchen's ongoing composition. The subtle vibration of the appliance transmitted through the floor, creating a physical dimension to its mechanical song.

Morning routines brought their own distinctive overture. The coffee maker performed its daily aria, beginning with the grinding of beans in sharp staccato bursts, followed by the gentle trickle of water through grounds, and concluding with the final hiss of steam. Toast popping up added sudden accents, while butter sizzling on hot bread created delicate crescendos of sound.

Knife work on the cutting board produced varying rhythms – the quick chopping of herbs, the measured slicing of vegetables, the heavy thunk of splitting squash. Each ingredient required its own cutting technique, creating distinct percussion patterns that echoed off kitchen walls. Metal utensils struck cooking surfaces with bell-like tones, while wooden spoons provided warmer, more muted notes.

The gas stove's burners played like wind instruments, their blue flames singing at different pitches depending on their intensity. Pots and pans conducted heat with their own voices – the sharp sizzle of searing meat, the gentle murmur of simmering sauces, the rolling boil of pasta water creating white noise rhythms.

Cabinet doors and drawers contributed their own section to the kitchen orchestra, each with a unique timbre based on its size and contents. The spice drawer rolled open with a rattle of glass bottles, while the pot cabinet produced deep, resonant tones. Measuring cups nested together with metallic rings, and mixing bowls stacked with hollow echoes.

The dishwasher cycled through its movement like a complex symphony, beginning with the rush of filling water, proceeding through various spray patterns, and concluding with the steam-release finale. Loading dishes created its own melody – the clink of glasses, the clatter of plates, the hollow thump of plastic containers finding their places in the racks.

Electric mixers added their mechanical voices to baking projects, changing pitch as they encountered resistance from thick dough or whipped cream. The oven's pre-heat cycle brought regular clicks as the temperature rose, while cooling fans hummed their steady notes. Timer beeps punctuated cooking intervals like conductors' cues, keeping multiple dishes orchestrated in perfect timing.

Fresh ingredients provided subtle acoustics – the snap of green beans being trimmed, the hollow thump of testing melons for ripeness, the crunch of lettuce being torn. Washing produce created water music in the sink, while the garbage disposal added brief but dramatic solos to the kitchen's performance.

Food storage containers conducted their own chamber music as lids were matched to bases, creating satisfying clicks and pops. Plastic wrap and aluminum foil unrolled with distinctive sounds, while resealable bags zipped shut with tiny linear crescendos. The pantry door's hinges creaked their own notes as ingredients were retrieved and returned.

Seasonal changes brought different instruments to the kitchen's ensemble. Summer canning operations filled the space with the ping of sealing jars and the bubble of boiling water baths. Winter holiday baking introduced the jingle of cookie cutters and the scrape of frosting spatulas. Spring cleaning produced the spray of cleaners and the squeak of cloths on surfaces, while fall preservation projects added the whir of food processors and blenders.

The microwave contributed its own electronic tones to the composition – the beep of buttons, the hum of the turntable, the final chime of completion. Its door latch clicked with mechanical precision, while the ventilation fan added a steady drone to busy cooking sessions.

Cooking mishaps introduced unexpected percussion – the clatter of dropped utensils, the sizzle of spills on hot surfaces, the quick scrape of burnt toast being rescued. These unplanned sounds added spontaneity to the kitchen's carefully conducted symphony, like jazz improvisations in a classical piece.

Recipe books ruffled their pages with paper whispers, while digital tablets chimed their wake-up tones. Measuring spoons jingled like tiny wind chimes as they were selected and used. The kitchen scale beeped its confirmations as ingredients were weighed, adding electronic punctuation to the cooking process.

Through the society's teachings, Sarah had learned to hear these kitchen sounds not as mere noise, but as an essential part of the culinary creative process. Each meal preparation became a unique performance, combining the voices of tools, ingredients, and cooking processes into a melodic dance of domestic creativity. The kitchen's symphony told stories of nourishment, experimentation, and the daily ritual of preparing food with care and attention.

Washing Machine Waltz

The laundry room's symphony began with the clink of quarters falling into the machine slot, a metallic prelude to the washing machine's elaborate performance. Sarah stood listening, remembering how the Ordinary Symphony Society had taught her to appreciate these mechanical melodies that most people ignored.

Each cycle started with the rush of water filling the drum, creating a liquid cascade that varied in pitch as the level rose. The initial splash against empty metal produced hollow echoes, gradually transforming into deeper, more resonant tones as clothes absorbed the water. Detergent powder scattered across wet fabric with a subtle hiss, while liquid soap created gentle plops as it joined the aquatic orchestra.

The agitator's movement established the primary rhythm, a steady back-and-forth motion that set the tempo for the entire wash cycle. Heavy loads of towels and jeans produced deep, rolling sounds, while lighter loads of delicates created softer, more delicate movements. The drum's rotation added its own layer of sound, a continuous revolution punctuated by the shift of wet fabric and the slide of buttons against metal.

Different fabrics contributed unique voices to the performance. Cotton items squeaked against the drum's surface, while synthetic materials created swishing sounds as they moved through the water. Zippers and buttons added percussion, clicking against the metal interior like tiny drumsticks. Velcro strips occasionally caught and released, creating sudden acoustic accents in the washing rhythm.

The spin cycle brought dramatic crescendos as the machine gradually increased its speed. Water extracted from the clothes sprayed against the drum in endless patterns, while the motor's pitch rose steadily higher. The machine's frame sometimes vibrated in sympathy, adding bass notes to the high-speed symphony. Unbalanced loads created their own unpredictable rhythms, forcing the machine to adjust and redistribute the weight.

Between cycles, the machine performed quiet interludes as water drained away with a gurgling diminuendo. The pause before the rinse cycle created moments of anticipation, broken by the sudden return of rushing water. Each rinse brought a cleaner sound to the water music, the soap-muffled tones giving way to pure liquid resonance.

The final spin reached the highest notes of the performance, the drum whirling at maximum speed while the last drops of water sprayed outward in centrifugal patterns. The motor's whine peaked and held, creating a sustained tone that filled the laundry room before gradually winding down to silence.

Multiple machines running simultaneously created complex harmonies, each at different points in their cycles. One might be in its gentle wash phase while another reached its spin crescendo, the overlapping rhythms creating an ever-changing laundry room chorus. The dryers added their own steady tumbling beats and warm air whoosh, complementing the washers' water music.

Maintenance sounds occasionally joined the performance – the squeak of belts, the click of timers, the subtle adjustments of aging machinery finding its balance. These mechanical voices told stories of well-worn parts and regular use, adding character to each machine's particular song.

The laundry room's acoustics enhanced certain frequencies while dampening others. Concrete walls reflected some sounds while absorbing others, creating a unique concert hall for these domestic instruments. The room's ventilation system provided a constant background drone, while the buzz of fluorescent lights added high harmonics to the mix.

Temperature variations affected the machines' voices. Hot water entering the drums created more steam and different resonances than cold water cycles. Winter months brought their own variations as heating pipes expanded and contracted, adding metallic pings to the laundry room's soundtrack.

Empty machines waited silently between uses, their still forms holding the potential for the next performance. The click of the door latch opening started each new concert, followed by the soft thump of clothes falling into the drum. Each load's composition was unique – the weight, material, and distribution of items affecting the sounds to come.

The society had taught Sarah to recognize the washing machine's cycles by sound alone. The gentle swish of the delicate cycle contrasted with the vigorous rhythm of heavy duty washing. Each program had its signature tempo and dynamic range, from the quick sports wash to the extended soak cycle.

Seasonal changes brought different compositions to the laundry room. Summer loads filled with light cottons and swimwear created different harmonies than winter's heavy sweaters and blankets. Spring cleaning introduced rarely-washed items with their own acoustic properties, while autumn brought the specific sounds of weather-resistant gear being prepared for winter.

Through careful listening, Sarah had learned to diagnose potential problems by subtle changes in the machines' songs. An unusual rattle might indicate a foreign object in the drum, while a change in the spin cycle's pitch could signal an unbalanced load. These mechanical melodies became a language of their own, communicating the health and function of each washer through its unique voice.

The washing machine waltz transformed mundane laundry tasks into musical experiences, each load an opportunity to appreciate the complex rhythms and harmonies of domestic machinery. The society had revealed how these everyday appliances performed their own special music, turning routine chores into concerts of water, motion, and mechanical precision.

House Whispers

Midnight brought a different kind of music to Sarah's home, a subtle symphony that the Ordinary Symphony Society had taught her to recognize. As the busy sounds of day faded, the house itself began to speak in whispers, telling stories through its settling foundations and aging materials.

The wooden floorboards conducted their nightly conversations, releasing the day's accumulated tension with soft creaks and gentle pops. Each board had its own voice, shaped by years of footsteps and seasonal changes. The oak planks in the hallway produced deep, resonant tones, while the pine in the bedroom offered higher, more delicate notes.

Radiators performed their thermal ensemble as they cooled, the metal contracting with periodic pings that echoed through the quiet rooms. Hot water pipes traced invisible paths through the walls, their cooling sounds mapping the house's circulatory system. In winter, the expanding and contracting of these mechanical arteries created a more elaborate performance, punctuated by the occasional knock of steam valves.

Windows participated in the nocturnal chorus, responding to temperature changes with subtle creaks in their frames. Old glass panes, slightly thicker at the bottom from years of gravity's pull, transmitted outside sounds with their own particular resonance. Wind moving past the house created varying tones as it encountered different architectural features – whistling softly around corners, humming through small gaps, and causing shutters to vibrate in their frames.

The attic space acted as a resonating chamber, amplifying and modifying sounds from below. Roof beams adjusted their ancient joints with wooden sighs, while insulation dampened some frequencies and enhanced others. During rainfall, the attic transformed into a percussion section, each droplet contributing to a complex rhythm on the shingles above.

Behind the walls, the house's infrastructure continued its constant work. Electrical wires carried their barely perceptible hum, while modern devices added their own electronic murmurs to the mix. The refrigerator's compressor cycled on and off in the kitchen below, its vibrations traveling through the structure like a distant heartbeat.

Doors and doorframes participated in the house's midnight sonata. Changes in humidity caused wood to expand or contract, creating subtle pressure between components. Some doors would softly click in their frames, while others remained silent partners in the architectural ensemble. Old hinges added their own aged voices, each with a distinctive pitch developed over years of use.

The basement contributed deep, resonant tones to the composition. Foundation walls responded to the earth's pressure with occasional adjustments, while support beams shared the weight of the structure above through barely audible shifts. The concrete floor acted as a drumhead, conducting vibrations from the ground and the house's movements.

Exterior siding played its part in the performance, responding to temperature changes with subtle expansions and contractions. Different materials created different sounds – wood clapboards produced organic creaks, while vinyl siding offered more synthetic clicks and pops. The house's corner boards served as junction points, mediating between different surfaces and their various acoustic properties.

Chimneys added their own voices when wind passed over their tops, creating gentle organ-pipe effects that varied with wind speed and direction. The flue damper might occasionally shift position with a metallic click, responding to air pressure changes or thermal movements.

The house's plumbing system performed its own nocturnal music. Water pressure adjustments caused pipes to flex slightly, producing muted tones within the walls. The hot water heater contributed periodic sounds as it maintained its temperature, while drain pipes carried occasional water sounds from upper floors.

Ceiling fixtures hung in silent anticipation of movement, though sometimes their chains or glass components would stir in response to air currents. Crown molding and baseboards marked the boundaries between surfaces, their joints occasionally releasing tension with small sounds that traveled along their length.

Weather changes brought special performances to the house's whispered symphony. Approaching storms could be heard in the building's reactions – subtle pressure changes that affected how doors closed, slight shifts in window frames, and variations in the usual creaks and settling sounds. The structure seemed to prepare itself for atmospheric changes, adjusting its components in anticipation.

Years of seasonal cycles had created well-worn paths for the house's movements, each sound marking a familiar adjustment in the building's constant process of settling and shifting. The society had taught Sarah to recognize these patterns, to understand which sounds were part of the house's normal operation and which might signal needed attention.

As Sarah lay in bed listening to these architectural whispers, she understood that her home was not simply a silent container for daily life, but a living, breathing entity with its own voice and rhythm. The house spoke of its history through these quiet sounds, each creak and whisper part of an ongoing dialogue between materials, time, and the natural forces that acted upon them. These midnight murmurs were the house's way of maintaining itself, adjusting to changes and releasing the accumulated tensions of another day in its long life.

Cooling Cabinet Blues

Beneath the kitchen's fluorescent glow, Sarah's refrigerator hummed its perpetual blues song, a performance that the Ordinary Symphony Society had taught her to appreciate in all its mechanical complexity. The appliance's steady baseline provided a constant rhythm to daily life, punctuated by the periodic clicks and whirs of its cooling system maintaining the perfect temperature.

The compressor served as the lead instrument, cycling through its repertoire with varying intensities. Its initial startup brought a deep, resonant tone that gradually settled into a consistent vibration. This mechanical heartbeat changed pitch slightly as the motor worked harder during hot summer days or when the door had been opened frequently, adjusting its efforts to maintain the cold environment within.

Ice formation created its own delicate music inside the freezer compartment. Tiny crystals grew with microscopic clicks, while the automatic ice maker performed its scheduled dance of filling, freezing, and releasing. Water flowing into the ice tray produced liquid notes, followed hours later by the sharp crack of ice breaking free and falling into the collection bin below.

The door seals conducted their own subtle symphony every time the refrigerator opened or closed. The magnetic gaskets released with a soft sucking sound, while closing produced a gentle whoosh of displaced air. Well-worn seals had developed their own particular voices, speaking of years of faithful service in maintaining the cold barrier between inside and outside.

Different compartments contributed unique acoustics to the performance. The crisper drawers slid with a smooth plastic glide, while glass shelves occasionally clinked against their supports when heavy items were placed or removed. The butter compartment's door closed with a distinct snap, and the egg tray created hollow echoes when eggs were retrieved for morning cooking.

Temperature variations between compartments generated their own sounds as materials expanded and contracted. The freezer section maintained its arctic environment with occasional creaks and pops, while the refrigerator portion adjusted more subtly to its milder climate. The division between these zones produced interesting harmonics as different materials responded to the temperature gradient.

The defrost cycle brought periodic interludes to the cooling cabinet's blues. Heating elements activated with a subtle electrical hum, gradually melting accumulated frost while fans circulated air to maintain temperature stability. Water droplets falling into the collection pan created random percussion, eventually evaporating in the warm air beneath the cabinet.

Storage containers added their voices to the composition. Glass jars clinked together when the door opened, while plastic containers rattled slightly on their shelves. Leftovers in covered dishes released small pops as their lids adjusted to pressure changes. The sound of containers being moved and rearranged became part of the daily rhythm of kitchen life.

The refrigerator's exterior surfaces acted as resonating panels, conducting and modifying its internal sounds. The side panels vibrated sympathetically with the compressor's rhythm, while the front face reflected kitchen sounds back into the room. Magnets and papers attached to the doors added their own subtle rattles to the mechanical chorus.

Seasonal changes affected the appliance's performance and its resulting soundtrack. Summer humidity created more condensation, leading to increased defrost cycles and water sounds. Winter's dry air produced different tones as the cooling system worked less intensively. Holiday periods brought fuller loads and more frequent door openings, changing the regular patterns of operation.

The freezer door's opening released clouds of cold air that fell to the floor with barely audible sighs, while warm air rushed in to replace it. Frost buildup changed the sound of the door seal, and ice cream containers produced distinctive scraping sounds as they were removed from their frozen storage.

Maintenance activities introduced new elements to the cooling symphony. Cleaning the condenser coils reduced the compressor's labored tones, while adjusting the temperature settings caused the control system to click through its range. Replacing water filters for the ice maker brought fresh clarity to its water music.

Power fluctuations created dramatic moments in the performance. Brief outages caused the compressor to restart with a flourish, while voltage variations affected the pitch of its operating hum. The electronic control panel added its own beeps and chimes to the mix, confirming temperature adjustments and announcing any issues requiring attention.

At night, when other kitchen sounds faded, the refrigerator's blues became more prominent. Its steady rhythm marked the passing hours, a mechanical lullaby that spoke of continuous operation and reliable service. The society had taught Sarah to hear these sounds not as mechanical noise, but as the voice of an essential household partner performing its vital role.

Through careful listening, she learned to recognize the subtle changes that might indicate needed maintenance or approaching problems. The cooling cabinet's blues told stories of food preservation, energy consumption, and the complex dance of temperature control that made modern kitchen life possible. Each click, hum, and whir contributed to an ongoing composition that played continuously in the background of daily life, keeping food fresh and families fed through its reliable performance.

Rain on Glass Sonata

Raindrops struck the windowpanes in an ever-changing pattern, each drop contributing its unique voice to nature's composition. Sarah sat by her bay window, remembering how the Ordinary Symphony Society had taught her to distinguish the intricate layers of sound in this liquid performance.

Large drops created bold, resonant tones as they struck the glass directly, while smaller droplets produced higher, more delicate notes. The angle of impact affected each drop's sound, with straight-falling rain delivering clear, distinct tones and wind-driven drops creating sliding effects across the glass surface.

The window's construction influenced its acoustic properties. Double-paned glass produced complex harmonies as drops struck the outer surface, their sounds modified by the air space between the panes. Old, single-pane windows offered more direct transmission of the rain's music, their thinner glass vibrating more readily with each impact.

Wind gusts orchestrated sudden crescendos, sending waves of droplets against the windows in rhythmic surges. These moments of intensity contrasted with quieter passages when the rain fell straight down, creating regular patterns of sound that seemed almost meditative in their consistency.

Temperature differences between inside and outside affected the acoustic experience. Warm rain falling on cool glass produced subtle variations in tone, while cold rain on heated windows created sharp, crisp sounds. Condensation forming on the interior surface added its own quiet counterpoint as tiny droplets merged and trickled downward.

The windows' metal frames conducted vibrations from the rain's impact, adding metallic overtones to the glass resonance. Corner joints and mounting points modified these vibrations, creating nodes of sound that varied depending on where the drops struck. Weather stripping dampened some frequencies while allowing others to pass through clearly.

Different windows around the house offered varying interpretations of the rain's music. North-facing windows received direct impacts during certain storms, while sheltered windows under eaves created more subtle performances. Bay windows provided multiple angles of sound, their divided panes producing a complex interplay of raindrop rhythms.

Storm intensity brought dramatic dynamic ranges to the performance. Light drizzle painted delicate patterns across the glass, each drop distinct and separate. Heavy downpours merged individual sounds into continuous streams of tone, punctuated by the occasional larger drop breaking through the general wash of sound.

The time of day influenced how the rain sonata was perceived. Morning rain caught early sunlight, adding visual sparkle to the acoustic performance. Night rain created a more intimate experience, with darkness focusing attention on the pure sound of water meeting glass. Dawn and dusk brought their own particular qualities to the rain's music.

Seasonal changes affected the character of the rain's performance. Spring rain fell soft and warm, while autumn storms brought harder, more dramatic impacts. Winter mixed rain with sleet and snow, creating complex rhythms as different forms of precipitation struck the windows. Summer thunderstorms delivered intense but brief performances, often accompanied by wind and electrical displays.

The glass itself acted as both instrument and amplifier, its surface tension affecting how drops spread and sound upon impact. Clean windows produced clear, bright tones, while dusty or dirty glass modified the sounds with subtle dampening effects. Recently cleaned windows seemed to sing with particular clarity, celebrating their renewed transparency with crisp, pure notes.

Surrounding architecture influenced how the rain sonata reached the listener. Overhanging roofs created protected zones where drops fell more softly, while open areas allowed full exposure to the rain's intensity. Nearby trees filtered and modified the rainfall, their leaves adding their own percussion to the overall composition.

Water running down the glass formed rivers and streams that modified incoming drops' sounds. These flowing patterns created continuous background tones that complemented the distinct impacts of new raindrops. The angle of the glass affected how these streams developed, with vertical windows producing straight channels and slanted surfaces creating meandering pathways.

The rain's rhythm often shifted unexpectedly, responding to unseen air currents and cloud patterns above. These changes brought fresh interest to extended performances, preventing the sound from becoming monotonous through constant variation in intensity and pattern.

Ground surfaces near the windows contributed their own elements to the composition. Rain striking puddles created counterpoint to the glass impacts, while drops falling on plants and soil added soft undertones to the overall sound. Paved surfaces produced sharp echoes that complemented the window's resonance.

Sarah had learned to appreciate how each rainstorm brought its own unique interpretation to this natural symphony. The society had shown her that these weren't just random sounds, but complex musical performances that deserved careful attention and appreciation. The rain on glass sonata played continuously through the seasons, each performance a reminder of nature's endless creativity in combining simple elements into extraordinary compositions.

Chapter 4: Urban Street Songs

Citys Industrial Symphony

Steel girders groaned against concrete foundations as the city awakened, its industrial heartbeat pulsing through Sarah's morning commute. The Ordinary Symphony Society had trained her ears to detect the intricate layers of urban music that most pedestrians ignored, treating each mechanical sound as part of a greater metropolitan composition.

Construction cranes pivoted overhead, their cables singing high-pitched melodies as they swayed in the morning breeze. Hydraulic lifts hissed pneumatic rhythms while elevating workers to upper floors, their mechanical arms extending and retracting in measured sequences. Welding torches sparked staccato notes that cascaded down steel frameworks, each spark contributing to the day's metallic chorus.

Subway trains rumbled beneath the streets, their vibrations traveling through underground tunnels and emerging as deep bass notes that resonated through manhole covers and grates. Steam vents released pressurized clouds with sudden hisses, creating periodic accents in the city's ongoing performance. The timing of these releases followed the hidden patterns of underground pressure systems, each vent adding its voice when conditions demanded.

Factory smokestacks conducted their own section of the industrial orchestra, releasing steam and exhaust in carefully regulated bursts. The sound of industrial fans created constant drone notes that varied with wind direction and speed. Cooling towers hummed their steady songs, their massive blades turning in slow, hypnotic rhythms that generated deep, persistent tones.

Loading docks contributed percussion to the symphony as metal plates rattled under the weight of forklifts and hand trucks. Pallets scraped against concrete floors, while hydraulic lifts on delivery trucks whirred and clicked through their cycles. The sharp impacts of heavy goods being moved created random rhythms that punctuated the steady flow of commerce.

Power transformers buzzed with electrical energy, their harmonics shifting as demand fluctuated throughout the day. High-tension wires overhead added faint, high-frequency tones that became more noticeable in humid weather. Emergency generators performed periodic testing routines, their diesel engines adding brief but powerful voices to the industrial chorus.

Conveyor systems in warehouses maintained steady rhythmic patterns as products moved through sorting and shipping processes. Rollers clicked against their supports while belt drives hummed at various frequencies depending on their loads. The occasional squeal of misaligned components added unplanned accents to the mechanical percussion.

Bridge traffic generated complex harmonies as vehicles crossed expansion joints in regular intervals. The weight and speed of different vehicles created varying tones, from the sharp reports of car tires to the rolling thunder of fully loaded trucks. Metal gratings sang distinct notes under each passing wheel, their pitch changing with temperature and wear.

Manufacturing plants contributed their specialized instruments to the performance. Stamping machines produced regular impacts that echoed through factory walls, while assembly line motors created continuous background tones. Robotic arms moved with precise timing, their servos whirring through programmed sequences that repeated with mechanical accuracy.

Ventilation systems served as the city's breathing apparatus, moving air through countless ducts and vents with steady determination. Massive HVAC units cycled through their heating and cooling programs, their compressors and fans working in coordinated patterns that changed with the seasons.

Ship horns from the harbor added their powerful voices to the industrial chorus, their deep tones carrying for miles across the urban landscape. Dock cranes performed their loading ballet, steel cables singing as containers were lifted and lowered in carefully choreographed movements.

Recycling centers created their own unique soundscape as materials were sorted and processed. Glass shattered with crystalline notes while cardboard was compressed with heavy hydraulic sighs. Metal scrap produced random percussion as it was moved and sorted, each piece contributing its particular tone to the recycling symphony.

The city's power plants maintained the underlying pulse of urban life, their turbines spinning with relentless precision. Cooling towers released steam with periodic whooshes, while coal conveyors added their steady rhythmic grinding to the industrial baseline.

Railroad yards orchestrated complex patterns of sound as trains were assembled and sorted. Coupling impacts created sharp percussive notes while diesel engines idled with deep, throaty rumbles. The screech of wheel flanges against rails added high-pitched accents to the railway chorus.

Sarah had learned to recognize how these industrial sounds changed throughout the day, reflecting the city's varying levels of activity. Morning brought the crescendo of starting machinery, while evening saw a gradual diminuendo as systems powered down. Night shifts maintained their own quieter rhythms, punctuated by the occasional surge of emergency vehicles or late deliveries.

The society had taught her that these mechanical sounds weren't mere noise but vital signs of urban health and activity. Each sound represented work being done, goods being moved, and services being provided. Together, they formed an industrial symphony that told the story of human ingenuity and determination, a constant reminder of the complex systems that kept the city alive and functioning.

Market Square Melodies

Vendors' calls echoed across the cobblestones as Sarah wandered through the morning market, each voice contributing to the rich tapestry of sound that the Ordinary Symphony Society had taught her to appreciate. The square pulsed with life, creating an ever-changing composition of human activity and commerce.

Fresh produce sellers arranged their displays with rhythmic precision, wooden crates scratching against metal stands while fruits and vegetables tumbled into precise pyramids. The snap of green beans being sorted provided crisp percussion, while the hollow thump of watermelons being tested for ripeness added bass notes to the morning chorus.

Fish mongers' voices carried across the square, their practiced calls rising and falling in traditional patterns passed down through generations. Ice crackled beneath fresh catches, and scaling knives created sharp, metallic rhythms against cleaning boards. The splash of water being thrown across fish displays added liquid notes to the market's soundtrack.

Bread vendors tapped fresh loaves, producing hollow percussion that spoke of perfectly baked crusts. Paper bags crinkled as warm pastries were wrapped, while coins clinked against ancient cash boxes in time-honored exchanges. The distant hum of bakery ovens provided a warm undertone to the morning's performance.

Coffee roasters contributed their aromatic percussion as beans tumbled in small-batch roasters. The hiss of espresso machines punctuated conversations, while ceramic cups clinked against saucers in countless impromptu cafes. Grinders whirred at varying pitches, each adjusting to its operator's precise specifications.

Flower sellers trimmed stems with sharp snips, dropping offcuts into buckets that resonated with each addition. Cellophane crackled as bouquets were wrapped, and water splashed as fresh flowers were arranged in metal buckets. The gentle rustle of petals in the morning breeze added subtle harmonies to the market's melody.

Cheese merchants cut through their wares with taut wires, creating soft whistling sounds that barely carried above the market's buzz. Wooden boards clunked against counter tops as samples were prepared, while wax paper sheets were torn with sharp efficiency for wrapping purchases.

Spice vendors scooped their colorful wares with metal spoons, creating delicate tinkling sounds as measures were poured into paper bags. Mortars and pestles ground custom blends with steady rhythms, releasing aromatic clouds that seemed to carry their own musical notes through the air.

The textile section rustled with activity as fabrics were unfolded and refolded in continuous motion. Scissors snicked through sample swatches, while measuring tapes snapped back into their cases with sharp retorts. Sewing machines added their mechanical percussion from nearby repair stalls.

Street musicians positioned themselves strategically around the square, their melodies weaving through the market's natural sounds. A violinist near the flower stalls played delicate phrases that complemented the morning's activities, while a guitarist by the cafe tables strummed chords that merged with conversation rhythms.

Children's voices darted through the soundscape like musical sparrows, their laughter and calls adding spontaneous joy to the market's composition. Parents' gentle warnings and encouragements provided counterpoint to their offspring's exuberance, creating familiar movements in the day's symphony.

Delivery trucks rumbled along the market's periphery, their engines providing bass notes as they supplied vendors with fresh stock. Hand trucks clattered across cobblestones while dollies squeaked under heavy loads. The metallic clang of delivery gates being raised and lowered marked time like orchestral cymbals.

Weather added its own elements to the market's melody. Awnings flapped in morning breezes while sun umbrellas creaked as they were adjusted throughout the day. Rain created entirely new movements in the market symphony, with droplets drumming on canvas covers and water rushing through ancient gutters.

The market clock tolled the hours with resonant authority, its sound carrying across the square to mark the passage of time. Each vendor seemed to know their part in this daily performance, their activities rising and falling in response to the clock's steady rhythm.

Seasonal changes brought variations to the market's melody. Summer crowds moved with languid ease while winter gatherings huddled more closely, their footsteps hurried against the cold. Spring and autumn each brought their own tempo to the square's activities.

Food court aromas seemed to carry their own musical notes as cooking sounds created percussion throughout the day. Woks clanged against burners while grills sizzled in steady rhythms. The clash of utensils and plates provided constant background percussion to the market's symphony.

Sarah had learned to hear how all these elements combined into a complex composition that celebrated daily life and commerce. The society showed her that markets weren't just places of transaction but venues for human interaction scored with countless overlapping sounds. Each visit revealed new layers in the market's endless symphony, a performance that had continued for generations and would persist as long as people gathered to trade, talk, and share their daily lives in this vibrant public space.

Chapter 5: Evening Sonata

Cutlery Concerto

Forks clinked against porcelain plates in the bustling restaurant, each impact contributing to an intricate percussion that Sarah had learned to appreciate through the Ordinary Symphony Society's guidance. The dining room resonated with metallic harmonies as hundreds of utensils performed their nightly ballet.

Soup spoons dipped into bowls with gentle precision, creating soft liquid sounds as they broke the surface. The return journey produced delicate drips that added staccato notes to the ongoing composition. When spoons touched bowl bottoms, they generated hollow tones that varied with each vessel's unique shape and material.

Knives scraped against plates in countless variations, their sounds changing with the pressure applied and the food being cut. Serrated blades produced rhythmic sawing notes while straight edges created smoother, continuous tones. The angle of contact affected each knife's voice, creating complex harmonies as diners worked through their meals.

Salad forks struck their tines against plates in light, high-pitched sequences. These smaller utensils produced more delicate sounds than their dinner counterparts, adding treble notes to the cutlery chorus. When tines scraped across plate surfaces, they created brief glissandos that slid through multiple pitches.

Water glasses joined the performance as they were lifted and returned to their places, each contact with the table producing crystalline notes that complemented the metallic symphony. Ice cubes clinked against glass walls, adding random percussion that changed as the cubes melted and shifted.

Serving utensils contributed deeper tones to the composition as they transferred food from platters to plates. Large spoons struck serving bowls with resonant authority, while carving forks stabilized their targets with muted metallic sounds. The scrape of serving spoons against casserole dishes created sustained notes that carried across the dining room.

Coffee spoons performed their own delicate movements, stirring with rhythmic precision as they clinked against cup sides. Sugar cubes dropped into cups produced bright splashes of sound, while spoons resting against saucers created occasional sharp notes when accidentally disturbed.

Bread knives serrated through crusty loaves, their saw-toothed edges producing complex harmonics as they worked. Butter knives spread their cargo with soft swooshing sounds, occasionally striking plates with quiet metallic points of percussion.

The kitchen's percussion section added background rhythms as cooks worked with larger utensils. Metal spoons struck pot sides during taste tests, while whisks created continuous scratching sounds against bowl surfaces. Spatulas scraped pans with authority, producing deeper tones that carried through serving windows.

Dessert forks and spoons introduced their refined voices later in the meal, their smaller sizes creating higher-pitched notes in the evening's ongoing performance. These specialized instruments often worked in pairs, creating counterpoint rhythms as diners tackled complex confections.

Children's utensils added unpredictable elements to the symphony, their plastic compositions producing softer, more muted tones. The random rhythms of learning diners contributed spontaneity to the otherwise orderly performance, while parents' correcting hands created syncopated patterns of guidance.

Wine glasses entered the composition with their own crystalline voices, stems touching down with delicate precision after toasts. The gentle impact of glass rims during celebrations added bright accent notes to the cutlery's steady performance.

Chopsticks contributed their unique percussion when in use, their wooden or bamboo construction producing warmer, more organic sounds. Their contact with ceramic bowls created hollow tones distinct from western utensils, adding cultural variety to the dining symphony.

The restaurant's surfaces affected each utensil's voice. Wooden tables dampened sounds while marble surfaces amplified them. Tablecloths muted percussion but enhanced sliding sounds as utensils moved across their fabric landscape.

Seasonal changes influenced the cutlery concert. Summer's lighter fare required gentler utensil work, while winter's heartier dishes demanded more robust cutting and scooping movements. Each season brought its own tempo and intensity to the dining room's performance.

Different courses created distinct movements in the meal's symphony. Appetizers began with light, delicate sounds that grew more complex during main courses. Dessert brought a return to lighter percussion as smaller utensils took center stage.

Service styles affected rhythm patterns throughout the room. Family-style dining created concentrated bursts of serving sounds, while course-by-course service spread utensil activity more evenly through the meal. Buffet service produced waves of percussion as diners returned to their tables in groups.

Sarah had learned to hear how each diner contributed their own part to this nightly performance. The society taught her that proper etiquette wasn't just about manners but about participating in a communal acoustic experience. Every meal became an opportunity to appreciate the complex choreography of countless utensils working in unconscious harmony.

The cutlery concert continued evening after evening, each performance unique yet following ancient patterns of human dining ritual. It celebrated the simple tools that accompanied every meal, transforming necessary actions into an ongoing symphony of silver, steel, and ceramic voices joined in the endless music of breaking bread together.

Living Room Orchestra

Leather creaked as Sarah settled into her favorite armchair, attuning her ears to the subtle symphony that the Ordinary Symphony Society had taught her to recognize in her own living space. The room's acoustic landscape revealed itself gradually, like musicians warming up before a performance.

The radiator began its morning overture with a series of gentle pings, metal expanding as warm water flowed through ancient pipes. Steam hissed softly through the valve, adding breathy notes to the household chorus. Each radiator section contributed its own voice, creating a thermal percussion section that marked the passing hours.

Wooden floorboards performed their aged choreography, responding to footsteps with distinctive creaks and groans. Each board had its own pitch, developed over decades of settling and wear. Temperature changes caused the wood to expand and contract, producing spontaneous notes throughout the day.

Window frames rattled gently in the breeze, while glass panes vibrated with passing traffic, creating tremolo effects that varied with vehicle size and speed. Curtains added soft rustling accompaniment as air currents moved through the room, their fabric creating delicate whispers against windowsills.

The grandfather clock in the corner maintained steady rhythm, its pendulum swinging with metronomic precision. Each tick marked passing seconds while hourly chimes added deeper, resonant notes to the room's ongoing composition. The mechanical whir of its winding mechanism created periodic interludes in the timekeeping performance.

Upholstered furniture contributed its own section to the orchestra. Couch springs squeaked quietly as weight shifted, while cushions released soft sighs when compressed. The leather armchair added creaking harmonies that changed with temperature and humidity, its material responding to every movement.

Picture frames tapped lightly against walls when doors closed, creating brief percussive accents. The ceiling fan's chain clinked against its housing in gentle metallic rhythms, while its blades created a steady whoosh that varied with speed settings.

Bookshelves added occasional commentary as their wooden surfaces expanded and contracted, producing soft creaks that seemed to emerge from nowhere. Heavy volumes shifted minutely, their leather bindings creating subtle sounds as they settled against each other.

The heating vent's metal grille rattled softly when the furnace activated, while rushing air created white noise that rose and fell with each cycle. Return air ducts added their own hollow resonance, completing the ventilation system's contribution to the domestic symphony.

Table lamps clicked as their switches were turned, their metal parts cooling and expanding with temperature changes. Lampshades occasionally brushed against bulbs, producing paper-like rustling sounds that punctuated quieter moments.

The fish tank's filter created a constant water melody, its steady flow punctuated by occasional bubbles rising to the surface. The aquarium's pump added a low hum that varied slightly as water levels changed, while the aerator created a gentle splashing percussion.

Potted plants participated with subtle movements, their leaves brushing against each other in response to air currents. Terracotta pots contributed hollow notes when watered, their porous surfaces absorbing moisture with quiet efficiency.

The cat's scratching post added random rhythms as claws worked against sisal rope, while the pet bed released soft whooshes as its occupant adjusted position. Food and water bowls created metallic notes when disturbed, marking feeding times throughout the day.

Electronics joined the performance with their own modern voices. The refrigerator's compressor cycled on and off in regular intervals, while the dishwasher added distant water music from the kitchen. Device chargers emitted barely perceptible hums that changed pitch as batteries approached capacity.

Doors throughout the house added percussion at irregular intervals. Hinges squeaked individual notes that identified each portal, while latches clicked with varying intensity. Door stops created spring-like bounces when struck, their coiled forms adding brief but distinctive sounds to the domestic chorus.

The coffee table's glass surface amplified sounds placed upon it, transforming ordinary activities into musical moments. Magazines created soft shuffling notes when moved, while coffee cups produced hollow tones against coasters.

Weather influenced the room's acoustic character throughout the year. Rain created gentle rhythms on windows and roof, while wind added whistling harmonies through weather stripping. Summer heat caused materials to expand and creak, while winter cold produced sharper, more brittle sounds.

Sarah had learned to appreciate how these domestic sounds combined into an ever-changing composition that reflected the life within her home. The society showed her that living spaces weren't merely silent containers but active participants in daily life, each room conducting its own orchestra of familiar sounds.

This living room symphony continued day and night, marking the passage of time with countless small voices joining in unconscious harmony. It created a sonic autobiography of the space, each sound contributing to the ongoing story of shelter, comfort, and domestic life that played out within these walls.

Night Pets Serenade

Moonlight filtered through the bedroom window as Sarah lay awake, listening to the nocturnal concert that the Ordinary Symphony Society had taught her to appreciate. Her cat, Mozart, began the evening's performance with a gentle purr that resonated at precisely 25 hertz, creating a bass line for the night's domestic symphony.

The neighbor's dog, a German Shepherd named Rex, contributed occasional deep woofs that carried through the quiet streets, each bark echoing off nearby buildings before fading into the darkness. These periodic announcements served as percussion in the nighttime orchestra, marking territory and time with equal dedication.

Crickets maintained their steady rhythm outside, their leg-rubbing sounds creating a continuous chorus that rose and fell with temperature changes. Each species contributed its own frequency, forming complex harmonies that shifted as different performers joined or left the ensemble.

An owl's hollow calls floated down from the old oak tree, its questions remaining unanswered yet adding haunting woodwind notes to the evening's composition. The sound carried particular resonance on still nights, when air density and temperature combined to perfect acoustic conditions.

Mozart's grooming routine added delicate percussion as rough tongue met fur in steady strokes. These quiet rhythms occasionally peaked with sudden scratching sessions, creating brief solos that punctuated the otherwise gentle performance. His claws created subtle scraping sounds against the carpet as he adjusted position throughout the night.

The aquarium's bubbler provided constant background texture, its gentle splashing mixing with the hum of the filter to create an aquatic ambient track. Neon tetras occasionally broke the surface tension, adding tiny splashes to the water's steady song.

Hamsters in their cages contributed randomized percussion as exercise wheels spun with varying enthusiasm. Water bottles released sporadic drops that clinked against metal tubes, while bedding rustled with continuous burrowing activities. Seed husks fell against plastic bottoms in quiet rainfall patterns.

The parakeet, though mostly silent at night, sometimes muttered dream-sounds that mimicked daily conversations. These sleep-talking episodes added unexpected vocals to the nocturnal symphony, complete with tiny beak clicks and wing adjustments that rustled against wooden perches.

Neighborhood cats conducted their own outdoor performances, their vocalizations ranging from gentle trills to passionate arias that echoed through empty streets. These feline operas often inspired indoor cats to add their own commentary, creating cross-species duets through window screens.

Small paws created subtle percussion across wooden floors as pets made their nightly rounds. Each animal's footsteps carried distinct rhythms - the measured pace of cats, the excited scampering of rodents, the cautious steps of elderly dogs. These movements formed a complex choreography of nocturnal patrol patterns.

The reptile terrarium's heat lamp clicked as its thermostat cycled, while its occupant, a leopard gecko, created soft sounds as it hunted crickets in the artificial twilight. Scales brushed against decorative rocks produced subtle scraping notes that barely registered above the ambient noise floor.

Outside, raccoons conducted percussion performances with metal trash cans, their dexterous paws creating unexpected rhythms as they searched for midnight snacks. These urban musicians often inspired chorus responses from neighborhood dogs, creating complex call-and-response patterns.

Moths bumped gently against window screens, adding random soft taps to the night's composition. Their wings created barely perceptible fluttering sounds as they danced around street lights, conducting aerial ballets to unheard music.

The guinea pig cage produced irregular rustling as its inhabitants rearranged their bedding, occasionally punctuated by the sharp squeak of social interactions. Their hay-chewing created continuous soft crunching sounds that marked their contentment with steady rhythm.

Fish tanks released occasional bubbles that broke the surface with quiet pops, while filter media trapped air pockets that escaped in irregular intervals. These aquatic sounds provided liquid texture to the otherwise dry acoustic landscape of the night.

Sarah had learned to distinguish individual voices within this complex arrangement - the specific tone of Mozart's purr, the unique cadence of each cricket, the particular resonance of every nocturnal visitor. The society showed her how these sounds combined into a living composition that celebrated the relationship between humans and their animal companions.

Dream whimpers from sleeping pets added emotional depth to the performance, their unconscious vocalizations suggesting adventures playing out in sleeping minds. Twitching paws kept time to unheard rhythms while whiskers quivered in response to phantom stimuli.

As night deepened, the symphony evolved. Early evening's energetic movements gave way to slower, more contemplative passages. Dawn's approach brought gradual key changes as diurnal creatures began stirring while nocturnal performers concluded their parts.

This nightly serenade continued year after year, each evening bringing slight variations to the eternal theme of coexistence between species. It celebrated the bond between humans and their animal companions, expressing through sound the complex relationships that filled homes with life, love, and endless music.

Warmths Whisper

Steam rose from Sarah's morning coffee, carrying with it the subtle sounds that the Ordinary Symphony Society had trained her to perceive. The gentle hiss of heated water molecules escaping into cooler air created a continuous treble note that changed pitch as the temperature gradually fell.

The old radiator in her kitchen joined the thermal chorus, its pipes expanding with quiet pings as hot water flowed through their metal chambers. Each joint and valve contributed unique tones to this morning overture, shaped by decades of mineral deposits and seasonal expansions.

Sunlight streaming through windows added its own silent warmth, causing window frames to expand with barely audible creaks. The greenhouse effect trapped heat in glass-enclosed spaces, creating gentle air currents that whispered against curtains and blinds.

The fireplace's burning logs performed a complex symphony of snaps and pops as moisture pockets exploded in the heat. Flames created soft rushing sounds as they consumed wood fibers, while ash settled with delicate sighs beneath the grate. The chimney added hollow resonance as it drew heated air upward, its draft creating a bass note that varied with wind conditions.

Her ceramic teapot released steam in rhythmic pulses from its spout, while its lid rattled softly as water reached rolling boil. The porcelain body transmitted heat-induced vibrations through its structure, creating microscopic movements that produced almost imperceptible sounds.

The oven's heating elements ticked as they expanded, their coils stretching minutely in response to electrical current. Heated air circulated through the cavity, creating soft turbulence that whispered against metal walls. The door's gasket compressed slightly as internal pressure changed, adding subtle squeaks to the thermal performance.

Hot water pipes throughout the house conducted their own temperature-based concert. Copper tubes expanded against support brackets, producing gentle creaks that traveled through wall spaces. Junction points between different materials created unique sounds as they accommodated thermal stress.

The coffee maker's heating element hummed at a specific frequency while maintaining optimal brewing temperature. Water bubbled through grounds with varying intensity, creating a liquid percussion that marked the extraction process. The warming plate beneath the carafe added its own gentle buzz to the morning's warmth-generated symphony.

Heated air rising from various sources created convection currents that moved through rooms with subtle acoustic effects. These thermal rivers carried sound differently than cooler air, bending acoustic waves in ways that changed how distant noises reached the ear.

The toaster's nichrome wires glowed and hummed as they transformed electrical energy into heat. Bread surfaces crackled softly as they browned, while the spring-loaded mechanism contained potential energy that released with a sharp snap when cooking completed.

Sarah's cast iron pan contributed its own thermal vocals as it heated on the stovetop. The heavy metal expanded gradually, sometimes producing sudden pings as molecular structures shifted. Food items added sizzling percussion when they met the hot surface, creating complex rhythms that varied with ingredient and temperature.

The microwave's turntable motor hummed while electromagnetic waves excited water molecules in food items. Steam escaped through plastic wrap with soft hisses, while heated containers released gentle pops as they expanded.

Sunlit windowsills created zones of thermal activity where house plants responded to warmth. Leaves unfurled with imperceptible movements, while soil released moisture that rose in silent columns. Terra cotta pots absorbed and released heat gradually, expanding and contracting with quiet mineral sounds.

The clothes dryer added its own warmth-generated acoustics to the domestic environment. Tumbling fabrics created soft rhythms while heated air rushed through the exhaust system. Metal surfaces pinged as they expanded during each cycle, marking time with thermal percussion.

Hot shower spray produced complex harmonies as water droplets struck surfaces at varying temperatures. Steam filled the bathroom space with its own acoustic properties, changing how sounds reflected from tiles and mirrors. The shower curtain moved gently in thermal currents, adding subtle rustling to the aqueous symphony.

The dishwasher's heating element warmed water to specific temperatures, creating underwater currents that moved through the machine with liquid music. Steam escaped through seals with gentle sighs during the drying cycle, while dishes clinked softly as they cooled.

Sarah had learned from the society that heat wasn't just a form of energy but a generator of subtle music that filled living spaces. Every warming element contributed its voice to an ongoing thermal chorus that marked the rhythms of domestic life.

Nighttime Rhythm

Darkness settled over Sarah's neighborhood as she tuned her ears to the evening's subtle percussion, guided by the lessons learned from the Ordinary Symphony Society. The night carried its own distinct tempo, slower and more deliberate than daylight hours, yet filled with intricate rhythmic patterns that emerged only after sunset.

Digital clocks throughout the house marked time with barely perceptible clicks, their LCD displays casting soft blue light that seemed to pulse with each passing minute. The old grandfather clock in the hallway maintained its steady beat, its pendulum swinging with metronomic precision through the quiet hours.

Traffic sounds changed character as evening progressed, transforming from rush hour's constant roar to isolated passages of individual vehicles. Each car created a unique doppler effect as it passed, its sound rising and falling in pitch while tires generated different frequencies on varying road surfaces.

The house's infrastructure maintained its own nocturnal rhythm section. The refrigerator's compressor cycled on and off at regular intervals, while the ice maker dropped fresh cubes into the bin with crystalline clicks. The heating system's fan created a baseline drone that ebbed and flowed with thermostat settings.

Wind played through trees outside, creating complex polyrhythms as branches swayed at different rates. Leaves rustled with varying intensity, while seed pods and pine cones occasionally dropped onto the roof, adding random percussive accents to nature's nighttime score.

The neighbor's motion-sensor light clicked on periodically, its relay creating a soft but distinct sound that preceded the subtle hum of illumination. Garden lights throughout the neighborhood switched on and off according to their timers, each adding their mechanical voices to the evening's technological rhythm.

Water moved through pipes with changing pressure as different households performed their nighttime routines. Shower spray from adjacent apartments created distant white noise, while drain pipes conducted liquid percussion through wall spaces. The water heater's burner ignited occasionally, maintaining temperature with a soft whoosh.

Insects maintained steady rhythmic backgrounds that varied by season. Crickets chirped at rates determined by temperature, while June bugs bounced against window screens in irregular patterns. Moth wings created subtle fluttering percussion as they danced around porch lights.

The cat's litter box auto-cleaner activated on schedule, its motor humming through a precise sequence of movements. Pet water fountains bubbled steadily, maintaining constant rhythms that encouraged nighttime drinking. Automatic feeders released kibble at programmed intervals, their mechanisms adding brief mechanical solos to the domestic symphony.

Sarah's bedside fan marked time with its rotating head, creating regular swells of white noise that swept across the room. Its pull chain tapped gently against the housing, adding metallic accents to the air movement's steady rhythm.

House timbers adjusted to nighttime temperature changes, producing occasional creaks that seemed random but followed predictable patterns of thermal contraction. Floorboards settled into their evening positions with subtle movements that responded to changing weight distributions as household members moved through their spaces.

The dishwasher's delayed cycle began its performance, water rushing through spray arms in precisely timed patterns while pump motors maintained steady baselines. Steam escaped through seals with regular sighs, marking progression through washing phases.

Window blinds responded to evening breezes with gentle tapping, their cords creating soft percussion against sills. Curtains moved in subtle patterns that matched air current rhythms, their fabric producing barely audible whispers against walls and windows.

Electronic devices throughout the house maintained their own electronic rhythms. Charging indicators pulsed with steady patterns, while standby lights created visual metronomes that matched their power-saving cycles. WiFi routers blinked in sequences that reflected data flow patterns.

The basement sump pump activated according to groundwater levels, its motor creating brief but intense rhythmic episodes that resonated through foundation walls. The water heater's anode rod released hydrogen bubbles in steady patterns, creating tiny percussive effects within the tank.

Distant train whistles carried through the night air at scheduled intervals, their doppler-shifted tones falling into familiar patterns that marked time on a larger scale. Airport flight patterns created recurring cycles of overhead sounds that followed strict timetables.

Sarah had learned to recognize these nighttime rhythms as essential elements of domestic life, each sound marking specific functions that continued through darkness. The society taught her that these mechanical and natural rhythms created a complex temporal framework that supported modern existence.

As midnight approached, the rhythm patterns shifted subtly. Some sounds decreased in frequency while others emerged to take their place, creating a graduated transition that carried through until dawn. These changes marked time's passage without need for clocks or schedules, maintaining order through acoustic patterns that remained consistent night after night.

Chapter 6: Weekend Rhapsody

Yard Work Symphony

Leaves crunched beneath Sarah's rake as she orchestrated her weekend yard maintenance, each sound carefully noted as the Ordinary Symphony Society had taught her. The metal tines created varying tones as they scraped across different surfaces - sharp and clear against concrete, muffled and rich across grass, scratchy and complex through fallen leaves.

The gas-powered mower contributed its distinctive baseline, its engine notes changing pitch as it encountered varying grass densities. The blade's rotation added a constant high-frequency whine that mixed with the lower engine tones, while clippings ejected from the side chute produced soft, irregular percussion as they settled onto the lawn.

Electric hedge trimmers performed their precise duet, each blade assembly creating synchronized sounds that varied with branch thickness. Young shoots produced high-pitched snips while woody stems generated deeper, more resonant cuts. The motor's pitch shifted under varying loads, creating a dynamic range of mechanical music.

The leaf blower conducted its own wind symphony, its adjustable nozzle producing different air frequencies as Sarah directed the flow. Leaves danced and swirled in the artificial breeze, adding their rustling voices to the mechanical chorus. The backpack-mounted motor transmitted vibrations that added physical percussion to the audio performance.

Pruning shears contributed punctuated solos with each decisive cut, their sharp blades meeting with satisfying clicks that changed tone depending on branch diameter. The bypass action created brief moments of tension before releasing with clean, crisp sounds that marked each finished cut.

Water spraying from irrigation heads produced complex harmonies as droplets struck various surfaces. Leaves responded with gentle pattering, while bare soil absorbed moisture with subtle hisses. Concrete pathways created sharper, more percussive notes as water bounced and scattered across their hard surfaces.

The wheelbarrow's single wheel generated changing frequencies as it rolled across uneven ground, its metal frame flexing and creaking under varying loads. Plant debris shifted and settled within the tub, creating organic percussion that marked each journey to the compost pile.

Garden tools clinked against each other in the tool belt, creating metallic rhythms that accompanied Sarah's movements. Trowels, pruners, and cultivators each contributed their distinctive tones to this portable percussion section, while fabric loops and leather holders added soft counterpoints.

The pressure washer's motor maintained a steady mechanical drone while its spray nozzle created sharp, focused sounds that changed with distance and angle. Water struck different surfaces with varying intensity, producing a range of tones that reflected each material's density and texture.

Birdsong provided nature's commentary on the maintenance activities, with different species responding to the mechanical sounds in their own ways. Some maintained distance and offered occasional critiques, while others swooped closer to investigate fresh-turned soil for exposed insects.

The compost tumbler creaked on its axis as Sarah rotated it, mixing fresh green material with decomposing layers. Contents shifted with muffled sounds that hinted at the alchemical processes occurring within, while the metal barrel generated hollow resonance with each turn.

Chain saw work added intense mechanical solos to the yard work symphony, its two-stroke engine producing complex harmonics that varied with load and chain speed. Wood fibers separated with distinctive sounds that changed with species and moisture content, while sawdust ejected in rhythmic pulses.

The string trimmer performed precision work around edges and obstacles, its rotating line creating sharp whines that modified pitch with varying resistance. Grass stems parted with subtle sounds while harder surfaces produced sharp impacts when contacted by the spinning filament.

Mulch spread from wheelbarrow to bed created soft shifting sounds as pieces settled into place. Each material type - wood chips, pine straw, or bark - produced unique acoustic signatures as it was distributed and arranged into protective layers.

Metal soil amendments clinked against spreading tools while organic fertilizers created softer sounds as they were distributed. Granules bounced across existing mulch layers with tiny impacts that multiplied into complex rhythmic patterns during broadcast application.

The garden hose contributed its own water music as pressure variations created different spray patterns. Adjustable nozzles produced everything from fine mists to concentrated streams, each setting generating distinct acoustic signatures as water met its targets.

Sarah had learned from the society that yard work created a unique symphony of purposeful sounds, each representing specific tasks that maintained outdoor spaces. These acoustic patterns marked seasonal changes and ongoing cycles of growth and maintenance that connected households to their environments.

As evening approached, power tools fell silent while natural sounds resumed prominence. The day's maintenance symphony concluded its performance, leaving behind subtle evidence of its passage - fresh-cut grass scent, newly trimmed edges, and cleaned surfaces that would slowly return to nature's preferred state until the next weekend's performance began anew.

This weekly orchestra of yard work represented humanity's ongoing dialogue with managed nature, creating rhythmic patterns that helped maintain order while acknowledging the constant flow of seasonal changes and growth cycles.

Retail Melodies

The automatic doors parted with their characteristic whoosh as Sarah entered the department store, her ears attuned to the retail soundscape as trained by the Ordinary Symphony Society. Overhead fluorescent lights hummed at specific frequencies, creating a constant electronic drone that formed the baseline for commercial spaces.

Shopping cart wheels produced varying frequencies as they rolled across different flooring materials. Smooth tiles generated steady rhythms while carpet sections muffled the sound, creating distinct acoustic zones that marked department boundaries. Squeaky wheels added their own distinctive voices to the rolling chorus.

Cash registers performed their monetary percussion with receipt printers chattering and cash drawers opening with sharp bell tones. Credit card readers beeped in confirmation while barcode scanners added their characteristic chirps to the transaction symphony. Coins clinked against each other as they were counted and distributed.

The produce section maintained its own specific soundscape. Misting systems activated at regular intervals, creating gentle water music while maintaining vegetable freshness. Shoppers selected fruits and vegetables, producing soft thuds and rustles as they tested ripeness and filled plastic bags.

Refrigeration units in dairy and frozen sections generated steady mechanical drones that varied by unit size and age. Door gaskets created soft suction sounds as shoppers accessed cold items, while frost-free systems cycled through their defrost sequences with subtle clicking and dripping sounds.

The deli counter's slicing machines whirred through their precise rotations, creating higher pitches when cutting through dense meats. Paper sheets rustled as orders were wrapped, while scales beeped as they displayed weights and prices. The plastic number dispenser clicked as customers advanced the queue.

Shopping bags crinkled and rustled as items were packed, their sounds varying with material and fullness. Plastic produced sharp crackles while paper generated softer, more organic tones. The rhythmic beeping of checkout scanners provided tempo for the bagging process.

Store announcements punctuated the ambient sound field at regular intervals, their compressed audio characteristics shaped by ceiling-mounted speakers. Pages for price checks and customer assistance created brief sonic interruptions that rippled through the retail space.

Metal shopping baskets stacked with metallic clinks, while plastic ones produced duller sounds as they nested together. The cart return area generated complex percussion as shoppers maneuvered vehicles into organized rows, metal frames contacting with varying force.

The bakery contributed warm sounds of cooling racks being filled and emptied, while plastic packaging crinkled as fresh items were wrapped. Bread slicers hummed through their precise cuts, and cabinet doors thumped softly closed after customers made their selections.

Conversation formed another layer of the retail symphony, its volume and character changing throughout the day. Morning shoppers spoke in hushed tones while afternoon crowds generated more energetic sound fields. Children's voices added bright, sometimes sharp accents to the acoustic environment.

The bottle return machine maintained its steady industrial rhythm, glass containers creating musical tones as they dropped into collection bins. Aluminum cans produced lighter percussion while plastic containers added hollow sounds to the recycling symphony.

Inventory restocking created its own nocturnal movements as pallets rolled across floors and cardboard boxes were opened with sharp blade sounds. Price tag guns clicked through their mechanical cycles while display racks were adjusted with metallic scrapes and clicks.

The customer service desk managed its own complex audio environment. Phones rang at varying intervals while returns were processed with scanner beeps and keyboard clicks. Gift cards activated with distinctive tones while lottery machines churned out tickets with mechanical precision.

Sarah had learned that each retail department maintained its unique acoustic signature. Electronics generated electronic sounds, fabric areas absorbed sound waves, while hardware sections produced metallic tones. These acoustic variations helped shoppers navigate spaces through unconscious audio cues.

Security systems added their subtle presence with door sensors chirping and surveillance cameras whirring as they tracked movement. Anti-theft devices created brief alarms when improperly deactivated, while security tags were removed with sharp clicking sounds.

The loading dock contributed distant industrial sounds as trucks arrived and departed. Hydraulic lifts whined under heavy loads while metal dock plates clanged into position. Pallet jacks rolled with characteristic squeaks as they transported goods from delivery to storage.

Weather influenced the retail soundscape as rain drummed on the roof and wind whistled through briefly opened doors. Climate control systems adjusted their output to compensate, adding varying fan speeds to the building's mechanical chorus.

The society taught that retail spaces created carefully orchestrated environments where commerce and sound intertwined. Each acoustic element served specific purposes while contributing to an overall atmosphere that encouraged shopping behavior.

As closing time approached, the sound field gradually transformed. Announcements became more frequent, customer voices faded, and cleaning equipment emerged to begin its evening performance. The day's retail symphony concluded its movement, ready to resume again with the next business day.

Playground Orchestration

Metal chains clinked rhythmically as children pumped their legs on swings, creating complex pendulum patterns that Sarah observed with newfound appreciation since joining the Ordinary Symphony Society. Each swing set produced its own distinctive tone, worn chains generating different pitches than newly installed ones, while rubber seat covers added subtle squeaks to the mechanical melody.

The spiral slide resonated with hollow sounds as children descended its curved path, their delighted squeals mixing with the plastic's vibrations. Static electricity created soft crackles during dry weather, while morning dew produced smoother, faster descents accompanied by different acoustic signatures.

Monkey bars rang with metallic notes as small hands grasped and released each rung. The hollow tubes produced varying tones depending on where they were struck, creating unintentional xylophones that contributed brief solos to the playground's ongoing performance.

Wood chip surfacing crunched underfoot with each step and landing, providing a constant percussion track that marked playground activities. The organic material shifted and settled continuously, its sounds changing with moisture content and compression patterns developed through regular use.

The seesaw's central pivot point creaked in steady rhythm as children balanced their weights, creating a mechanical metronome that marked time in the play space. Each end produced soft thuds as it contacted ground-mounted tire bumpers, while riders adjusted positions with shuffling sounds.

Spring riders squeaked through their bouncing arcs, each animal-shaped seat producing unique sounds based on age and maintenance. Metal coils compressed and released with varying tension, creating distinctive notes that changed with rider weight and movement intensity.

The climbing dome generated complex harmonics as multiple children navigated its geometric framework. Metal joints flexed and vibrated while rubber-soled shoes squeaked against painted surfaces. The dome's hollow structure amplified and transformed these sounds into resonant tones.

Basketball courts contributed their own rhythm section as balls bounced against asphalt with regular impact sounds. Chain nets added metallic whispers to successful shots, while backboards produced deep, reverberating booms when struck directly. Sneakers squeaked against playing surfaces as children changed direction.

The sandbox maintained softer acoustics as plastic shovels scraped against grain surfaces and small buckets filled and emptied with gentle shifting sounds. Sand cascaded in varying streams, creating subtle white noise that changed with moisture content and pouring height.

Merry-go-rounds spun with distinctive mechanical sounds, their central bearings producing varying pitches that reflected rotation speed. Handholds rattled with subtle metallic notes while centrifugal force pulled riders outward, their laughter mixing with the spinning symphony.

Children's voices wove through all these mechanical sounds, creating a dynamic vocal layer that shifted constantly in pitch and intensity. Shouts of excitement, calls to friends, and occasional tears all contributed to the playground's emotional soundscape.

The fence surrounding the play area rattled with metallic notes when struck by stray balls or leaned upon by resting children. Chain link sections produced varying tones depending on tension and post spacing, while gate hinges added their own creaking voices.

Rubber mat surfaces beneath equipment generated muffled footfalls that contrasted with surrounding materials. The specialized surfacing created acoustic zones that marked safety areas while producing distinctive sounds during impacts and landings.

Weather conditions altered the playground's acoustic character throughout seasons. Rain created new percussion on metal surfaces while adding slick textures that modified play sounds. Wind whistled through equipment frameworks and set chains swaying with gentle clicks.

Parents' conversations formed another audio layer, their adult voices maintaining steady background tones that anchored the more chaotic children's sounds. Warnings, encouragement, and casual discussion blended into a constant vocal foundation.

The drinking fountain contributed its periodic water music as children hydrated between activities. The button's mechanical click preceded each water stream, while drain sounds provided bass notes to the brief liquid interlude.

Bicycle racks created occasional metallic percussion as riders secured and retrieved their transportation. Locks clicked through combination sequences while kickstands scraped against concrete with characteristic sounds.

The society taught Sarah that playgrounds represented unique acoustic environments where mechanical sounds merged with human activity in constantly changing patterns. Each equipment piece contributed specific tones while supporting physical development and social interaction.

Maintenance activities added their own periodic sounds to the playground symphony. Bolts tightened with ratcheting clicks, chains lubricated with subtle changes to their operating sounds, and surfaces cleaned with scraping tools all marked ongoing care routines.

As evening approached, the playground's acoustic energy gradually diminished. Individual equipment voices became more distinct as fewer children played, while longer shadows changed the space's acoustic properties. The day's performance wound down until only wind-driven sounds remained, waiting for the next day's playground symphony to begin anew.